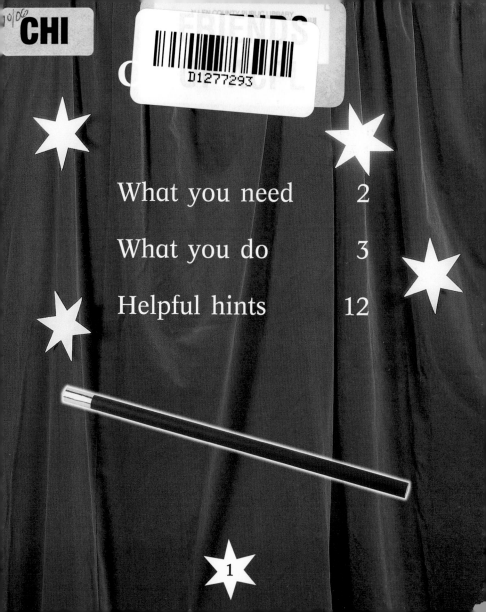

1

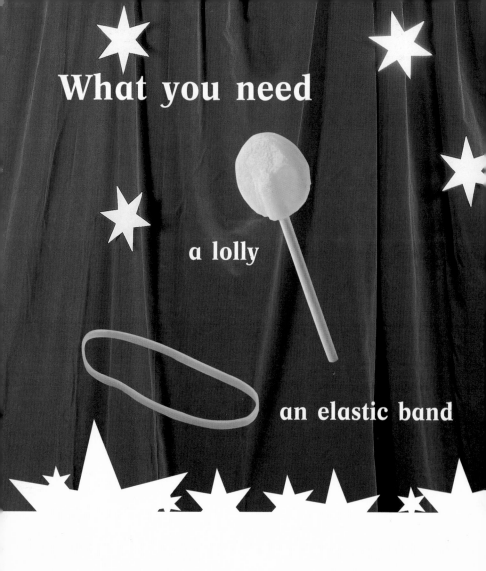

What you need

a lolly

an elastic band

What you do

No, *not* like this!

No, *not* like this!

Yes, like this!

Put the elastic band on your finger.

Put the lolly in the elastic band.

No, *not* like this!

Yes, like this!

When you do the trick,

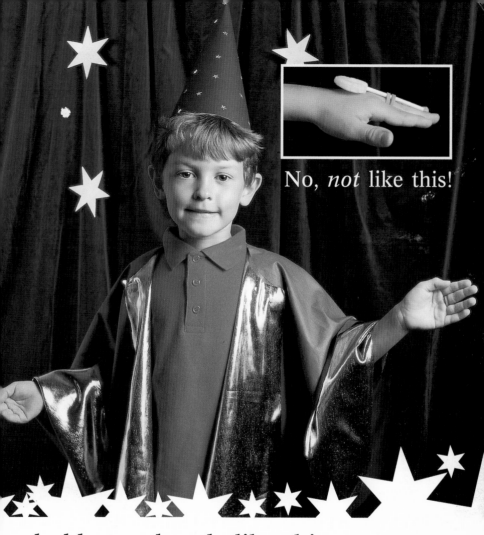

No, *not* like this!

hold your hands like this.

Wave your hands.

Make a fist.

Grab the lolly.

Yes! It's magic!

Helpful hints

★ Use an elastic band which is the same colour as your skin.

★ Don't show the lolly to the audience until the end of the trick.

★ As you do the trick, talk to your audience. You could say, "Ladies and gentlemen, I have nothing in my hands!"

★ Keep your hands moving as you wave your arms and grab the lolly. Don't stop or slow down because the audience will see what you are doing.

★ Try giving the lolly to someone in the audience. If you do, hide the hand with the elastic band.

★ Never tell anyone how you do your tricks!

★ Practise, practise and practise again!